Bible Studies

PRACTICAL PRAYER

Bible Studies

PRACTICAL PRAYER

JOSEPH YOO

Abingdon Press
Nashville

PRACTICAL PRAYER
CONVERGE BIBLE STUDIES

By Joseph Yoo

Library of Congress Cataloging-in-Publication Data has been requested.

ISBN: 978-1-4267-7825-4

Series Editor: Shane Raynor

13 14 15 16 17 18 19 20 21 22—10 9 8 7 6 5 4 3 2 1

Manufactured in the United States of America

CONTENTS

ABOUT THE SERIES

Converge is a series of topical Bible studies based on the Common English Bible translation. Each title in the *Converge* series consists of four studies based around a common topic or theme. *Converge* brings together a unique group of writers from different backgrounds, traditions, and age groups.

HOW TO USE THESE STUDIES

Converge Bible studies can be used by small groups, classes, or individuals. Each study uses a simple format. For the convenience of the reader, the primary Scripture passages are included. In Insight and Ideas, the author of the study guide explores each Scripture passage, going deeper into the text and helping readers understand how the Scripture connects with the theme of the study. Questions are designed to encourage both personal reflection and group conversation. Some questions may not have simple answers. That's part of what makes studying the Bible so exciting.

Although Bible passages are included with each session, study participants may find it useful to have personal Bibles on hand for referencing other Scriptures. Converge studies are designed for use with the Common English Bible; but they work well with any modern, reliable translation.

ONLINE EXTRAS

Converge studies are available in both print and digital formats. Each title in the series has additional components that are available online, including companion articles, blog posts, extra questions, sermon ideas, and podcasts.

To access the companion materials, visit

http://www.MinistryMatters.com/Converge

Thanks for using *Converge*!

INTRODUCTION

As a pastor's kid, I grew up in a family that emphasized the importance of prayer. My father always seemed to be at church praying. Sometimes he'd go early in the morning before the sun rose. Other times, he'd go late at night. He taught me, both by word and example, how important prayer is to our lives. He showed me that prayer is where real ministry begins to happen.

On paper, praying seems easy enough. All it involves is taking a few minutes here and there to talk to God. How hard could that be, right? But when we try to pray daily, we realize that it's much harder than we'd thought. It's usually easier to come up with excuses *not to* pray than reasons *to* pray. And the most common excuse seems to be the busyness of life.

Pastor and author Bill Hybels has written that "information about prayer is important, but it will do us no good if we never slow down long enough to pray. And most of us are far too busy for our spiritual health." I have taken that to heart, but it's something that I still struggle with—not in a theological sense but in a practical sense. It's hard to be intentional about prayer because it's so much easier to get carried away with my daily activities and routine.

Every morning, when I get to work, I want to—I *intend* to—begin my day with prayer and a short devotional so that I can start things off on the right foot. But more often than not, I'm unsuccessful.

When I get to my church office, . . .

> . . . There's a memo asking for a return call.
> . . . The phone is alerting me that I have voicemail.
> . . . My inbox is gently letting me know that it needs to be purged.
> . . . There's just too much clutter on my desk for me to concentrate.
> . . . The office is too darn cold.
> . . . There are one too many spiders on my desk and in my office—a huge threat to my sanity and safety. (I am not a fan of spiders. I'm being nice when I say that.)

I know that I should just ignore it all and get to praying. Everything will all still be there after my time with God. But I feel so distracted. I want to have a clear mind before communing with God. So I start on a slippery slope by saying to myself:

> . . . Let me listen to this voicemail just to see who it's from.
> . . . Let me browse through my e-mail to see whether there's anything urgent.

. . . Let me put these books away. But wait! Why were they on my desk? I should browse through them to see whether I can remember why I left them on my desk.

. . . It's freezing in here! Where's my jacket? Why isn't the heater working?

. . . Wow, that's a huge spider! I think I'm going to call it a day and not come back to the office until someone takes care of that spider.

One thing leads to another; and the next thing I know, it's time for that late-morning meeting. Then lunch. Then an afternoon meeting. Later that night, as I'm lying in bed, I suddenly remember that I forgot to pray in the morning.

"Shoot, I did it again! Geez! OK. Tomorrow, definitely tomorrow. I'll pray to start off my workday."

I'm actually shocked and embarrassed by how easy it is not to pray. And if I'm not careful, it's quite possible to go a very long time without praying.

Surely, I can't be the only one who struggles with this!

I know that if I'm too busy to pray, then something in my life is out of whack. Usually, it means I need to reorganize my priorities around God.

In no way am I an expert on prayer. I just shared with you my struggles in making prayer a disciplined habit for my mornings. I feel a bit overwhelmed and amateurish as I share this study with you because I don't know whether I can offer you any insights or new thoughts on this vital ingredient of our faith journey. In fact, it's very likely that you may have more insights on prayer than I do.

My hope for this study is that you and I will be reminded of just how vital prayer is to our faith journey. However, knowing and doing are completely different things; and I want to move from knowing to practicing and doing.

We'll begin with why we need to pray in the first place. Then we'll talk about whether there's a wrong way to pray. In the third session, we'll spend some time on why God doesn't seem to answer our prayers. Finally, we'll take a look at the importance of listening to God's voice.

I pray that these four sessions will help start discussions about prayer with your friends, family, and community.

May prayer become an ever-increasing part of our faith and lives!

1

WHY WE PRAY
GETTING TO KNOW GOD'S HEART

SCRIPTURE
LUKE 6:12-19; 1 THESSALONIANS 5:12-24

LUKE 6:12-19

[12]During that time, Jesus went out to the mountain to pray, and he prayed to God all night long. [13]At daybreak, he called together his disciples. He chose twelve of them whom he called apostles: [14]Simon, whom he named Peter; his brother Andrew; James; John; Philip; Bartholomew; [15]Matthew; Thomas; James the son of Alphaeus; Simon, who was called a zealot; [16]Judas the son of James; and Judas Iscariot, who became a traitor.

[17]Jesus came down from the mountain with them and stood on a large area of level ground. A great company of his disciples and a huge crowd of people from all around Judea and Jerusalem and the area around Tyre and Sidon joined him there. [18]They

came to hear him and to be healed from their diseases, and those bothered by unclean spirits were healed. [19]The whole crowd wanted to touch him, because power was going out from him and he was healing everyone.

1 THESSALONIANS 5:12-24

[12]Brothers and sisters, we ask you to respect those who are working with you, leading you, and instructing you. [13]Think of them highly with love because of their work. Live in peace with each other. [14]Brothers and sisters, we urge you to warn those who are disorderly. Comfort the discouraged. Help the weak. Be patient with everyone. [15]Make sure no one repays a wrong with a wrong, but always pursue the good for each other and everyone else. [16]Rejoice always. [17]Pray continually. [18]Give thanks in every situation because this is God's will for you in Christ Jesus. [19]Don't suppress the Spirit. [20]Don't brush off Spirit-inspired messages, [21]but examine everything carefully and hang on to what is good. [22]Avoid every kind of evil. [23]Now, may the God of peace himself cause you to be completely dedicated to him; and may your spirit, soul, and body be kept intact and blameless at our Lord Jesus Christ's coming. [24]The one who is calling you is faithful and will do this

INSIGHT AND IDEAS

During my college days, seven friends from high school and I spent a lot of time hanging out together. There were four guys and four girls in our group. We guys lived in a campus apartment together, and the girls lived in the apartment right above ours. We'd try to eat together as much as possible throughout the week (mostly to save money); but once a week, we'd have a "family dinner."

There was one member of our group who constantly talked about herself and her problems, mainly about the guys she was seeing. At first, we were genuinely interested in helping her make the right decisions and so forth. But every time we got together, we heard about how so-and-so was calling some other girl, all while he was supposed to be seeing her. Yada, yada, yada.

What's worse was when we tried to share with her the struggles that we were experiencing, she'd hijack the conversation. "Oh, I know! Michael did the same thing to me. Well, not really the same thing, but you know, close enough." But it never really was "close enough" to what we were talking about. Nevertheless, on and on she would go.

Sometimes she would call one of us to ask whether we could get coffee or lunch and hang out and talk. Again, at first, all of us were more than eager to skip out on studying or doing school-related things to spend time with a friend. Especially me. I always looked for ways to avoid my college responsibilities. But I quickly learned that our conversations always ended up being about her problems.

Slowly, we guys began to pull away from her. It was easier for us to do this than it was for the girls, because we didn't live in the same apartment. Things reached the point that if we knew that she was going to be present, we'd hold minor competitions where the winner would be excused from hanging out with the entire group. For some odd reason, our group almost always did things together. I think that it was because, secretly, we were scared of the girls, although none of us would admit it.

During our weekly "family dinners," we would eat, clean up, and get out of Dodge as quickly as possible, making up excuses if necessary.

We even entered her in our cell phone contacts as "Do Not Answer" so that when the phone rang, we'd be able to avoid talking to her. Of course, this wasn't a very mature or gracious way to handle the situation. But we were young. And we were boys who were a bit on the slow and immature side. Every time she called, she seemed to be wanting something from us. And when we didn't answer, she'd confront us and ask why. This infuriated us, because she would never answer when we called her. Ever. I swear her phone only made outgoing calls.

Truthfully, we were just tired of dealing with a one-sided relationship. We could never bounce ideas off of her, we could never share our stories or our days with her, and we could never talk about our struggles and problems because she would always turn the conversation around and make it about herself.

Most of us probably know people like that—those who keep taking and taking but are never able to give. If you don't have anyone like that in your life, there's a good chance that you might be that person. Of course, I'm kidding.

MORE THAN JUST SUPPLICATION

Our relationship with God can sometimes become one-sided too, especially if we carry a narrow view of prayer. Some of us see prayer mostly as a time of supplication, where we come before God and ask for things. Or we make it the "break in case of emergency" part of our faith journey, where it's the last resort we take—a form of bailout that we desperately seek from God. So when we hear people say things like, "Pray continually," it may be difficult for us to understand why, because most of the time, we don't need to be rescued. And there are points in our lives when everything is going decently to great. It's common to forget to pray during those times.

If this is how we approach prayer, it's possible that we have a limited view of God as well. If our prayers are nothing more than a wish list, perhaps we view God as someone like Santa Claus. We figure that the better we behave, the more we go to church, the more we follow God's commandments, and so forth, the better chance we have that our prayers will be answered. Essentially, we become like that person from my college days—only approaching God when we need something. But while asking God for help and grace is an important part of prayer, it's just that—a part of prayer.

A pastor once told me that breathing is to the body as prayer is to the soul. Prayer is not just something that we do before we consume a meal. Or something we do before we take a test that we didn't study for. Or a plea bargain we make after breaking Mom's treasured vase. You know how it goes: "God, if you fix this right now, I'll be nice to my brother from now on. Not just for today. Not just for this month. But forever. I'll be really nice to him." Or "If you can make my mom never find out about this, I'll never hit my brother again. Ever. Please help. Amen." Not that I'm speaking from experience.

Prayer is so much more than us just yelling, "Help!"

COMMUNICATION AND RELATIONSHIP

Early in my faith formation, a youth pastor told me that the biggest difference between Christianity and other religions is that, in Christianity, God wants to have a relationship with us. With me. This was such a foreign (and fantastic) concept for me at the time. A relationship? With me? God? Wow! It changed the way I viewed God. And it was probably the point where I began to take ownership of my faith rather than thinking that I had inherited God from my dad (who happens to be a pastor).

Practically anyone, from professional counselors to those who have been married for years will tell you that the most important part of a relationship is communication. If you don't communicate, problems will arise. Prayer is how we communicate with God. If we limit our communication with God to only wish lists and requests for help, we're limiting our relationship with God as well. It's hard to have a full relationship with people in our lives who just want something from us. And it's hard for people to have a relationship with us if all of our communication is our asking them for something. This is how prayer works, too.

Not that we can really have a "balanced" relationship with God. After all, God is the Creator; we are just the creation. But that shouldn't stop us from attempting to have the fullest relationship with God that we can possibly have.

WE PRAY SO WE CAN HEAR GOD

In prayer, we commune with God. We thank God. We bless God. We adore God. We praise God. We confess to God. And we ask God for help.

When it comes to prayer, we Koreans have a beautiful and powerful tradition called *tongsung kido*. We all say our individual prayers out loud, all at once.[1] But prayer is so much more than just talking.

During a youth retreat, I once witnessed a student who was pouring out her heart in prayer. For some reason, I could sense a bit of frustration in her words. As the prayer time went on, she got louder and louder, sounding more and more frustrated. Afterward, I pulled her aside and said, "Hey, I don't know what you're praying for; but next time during worship, when we pray, instead of going on and on

---

1 For an example of *tongsung kido*, visit *http://youtu.be/9jpavBmiPVg*. Praying begins at 0:26.

in your prayers, take time to just listen. Sit back. Ignore all the other sounds going on, and try to prayerfully listen. I don't know if that'll help you or change anything, but I felt like I should let you know that."

The next day, she came to me and said, "Thanks, I feel so much more at peace. I think I was talking too much to hear from God."

Listening is an important part of prayer, too. In fact, it's an important aspect in all of our relationships. Communication is a two-way street, and it's practically impossible to hear God if we aren't actively listening for God's voice.

PRAYER SUSTAINS US

Throughout the four Gospels, there are many mentions of Jesus withdrawing and spending time in prayer with God. I believe that it was these times spent in prayer that really sustained Jesus. His prayer life gave him strength, refreshed and renewed him in his ministry; and most important, it helped him stay in tune with God. Jesus modeled an intimate relationship with God; and this intimacy had a lot do with how much time he spent in prayer, often withdrawing from everyone else.

If Jesus found it important to pray—to intentionally carve out time dedicated to prayer—then it should be a high priority for us too.

In our close relationships, we often know what our best friend or our spouse or significant other is thinking because of how much time we spend together talking and listening to one another. Much like that, the more time we spend with God in prayer, the more we understand what God's purpose for our life is. The more we pray, the more we get to know God's heart. The more we pray, the more we know God's will. The more we pray, the more we're in tune with God.

Prayer is not just about getting God to do what we want or need. Prayer is more about getting ourselves to do what God wants us to. Nineteenth century Danish theologian Søren Kierkegaard said it perfectly: "The function of prayer is not to influence God, but rather to change the nature of the one who prays."

So, we pray—not only to ask God for help but also to offer our thanks. We pray to praise and adore God. We pray to confess our shortcomings to God. We pray to commune and communicate with God. We pray so that we become more and more in tune with God.

May we all shape our prayer lives to become more than just asking for help. May we learn to listen, talk, reflect, and just be in God's presence.

May we, like our Christ, find time to intentionally be in prayer.

May we see that prayer is more than just an act that we engage in here and there, but that it's a way of living.

And may we pray continually.

QUESTIONS

1. Why did Jesus pray all night (Luke 6:12)? Do you think that this was a regular habit? Is this something that believers should try to imitate? Why, or why not?

2. What was the point of Jesus' going to the mountain to pray (Luke 6:12)?

3. What was the connection between Jesus' prayer and the power that was going out of him to heal the sick and those bothered by unclean spirits (Luke 6:19)?

4. Did Jesus really need to pray? Why, or why not?

5. What does it mean to rejoice always (1 Thessalonians 5:16)? What are some strategies for doing this? Why is it important?

6. What does it mean to pray continually (1 Thessalonians 5:17)?

7. What is the connection between prayer and giving thanks (1 Thessalonians 5:18)?

8. First Thessalonians 5:19 instructs us not to suppress the Holy Spirit. Is it possible to suppress the Spirit when we pray? How do we keep from doing this?

9. How does prayer help us avoid evil (1 Thessalonians 5:22)?

10. What role should supplication (requesting things from God) play in our prayers?

11. Why is listening so important in prayer? How do we learn to listen more?

12. How does prayer contribute to a healthy relationship with God? What does it mean to be intentional in praying?

13. Do you agree or disagree with the Søren Kierkegaard statement that "the function of prayer is not to influence God"?

2

HOW WE PRAY
LEARNING TO COMMUNICATE WITH GOD

SCRIPTURE
MATTHEW 6:1-15

[1]"Be careful that you don't practice your religion in front of people to draw their attention. If you do, you will have no reward from your Father who is in heaven.

[2]"Whenever you give to the poor, don't blow your trumpet as the hypocrites do in the synagogues and in the streets so that they may get praise from people. I assure you, that's the only reward they'll get. [3]But when you give to the poor, don't let your left hand know what your right hand is doing [4]so that you may give to the poor in secret. Your Father who sees what you do in secret will reward you.

[5]"When you pray, don't be like hypocrites. They love to pray standing in the synagogues and on the street corners so that

people will see them. I assure you, that's the only reward they'll get. ⁶But when you pray, go to your room, shut the door, and pray to your Father who is present in that secret place. Your Father who sees what you do in secret will reward you.

⁷"When you pray, don't pour out a flood of empty words, as the Gentiles do. They think that by saying many words they'll be heard. ⁸Don't be like them, because your Father knows what you need before you ask. ⁹Pray like this:

Our Father who is in heaven,
    uphold the holiness of your name.
¹⁰Bring in your kingdom
    so that your will is done on earth
    as it's done in heaven.
¹¹Give us the bread we need for today.
¹²Forgive us for the ways
    we have wronged you,
just as we also forgive those
    who have wronged us.
¹³And don't lead us into temptation,
    but rescue us from the evil one.
¹⁴"If you forgive others their sins, your heavenly Father will also forgive you. ¹⁵But if you don't forgive others, neither will your Father forgive your sins.

INSIGHT AND IDEAS

We Koreans seem to have a flair for the dramatic. Yes, I realize that this is a very broad, general, and maybe even unfair statement.

Once during a Sunday morning service at a Korean church, an elder of the church was going to do the morning prayer. He methodically and gracefully walked to the pulpit, paused for a few seconds, cleared his throat, and began to pray softly.

The words and phrases he was using felt like the Korean equivalent of the words and phrases found in the King James Bible, meaning that no one, not even he, spoke that way in the real world. As the prayer went on (and on), he became louder and more convicted. As his volume increased and as he displayed more passion, his voice would quiver and tremble at the end of each phrase.

I couldn't hold my curiosity any longer; I just had to see how he looked as he prayed. His eyes were tightly shut, creating even more wrinkles. Both arms were raised above his head, pumping them to accentuate the words he was unleashing. He reached the climactic point of his prayer and took a long, dramatic pause. Then, in a very soft, trembling, fear-filled voice, he whispered, "In Jesus' name" (another pause), "we pray. Amen."

I felt that all that was missing from this prayer was a single tear rolling down his cheek.

What made it worse was that this man wasn't the nicest of people. He usually gave everyone a hard time. No one was to question him or his motives, ideas, suggestions, critiques. He wanted everyone to know who he was and the "high" and "honorable" positions he held within the church. And all of those who were younger than he had better be good Koreans and respect authority (read: Don't question; just do as he says). So for him to stand and pray like that, on behalf of the church, well, it felt . . . empty. It seemed like he was putting on a show.

Now, I know that I probably sound very snarky and judgmental with this story. But the worship service that morning raised another issue, one that bothered me even more than the man's prayer did.

PRAYER OBSTACLES

After quite a few (both private and group) conversations with some youth who were present, I learned that many of them felt like they didn't know how to pray. They thought that Christians had to pray the way the elder prayed in front of the church in both private and public prayer.

They felt that they didn't know enough fancy words to use during prayer.

They felt that they hadn't memorized enough Bible verses to quote during prayer.

They didn't know how to "speak in tongues," as many of the adults did during prayer.

28

They felt that they didn't know how to "perform" (for a lack of a better word) like the elder did in his prayer.

They simply chose not to pray.

"I don't know how to pray the right way, so I just . . . I just don't," one youth shared with me.

"I've been asking God for the gift of tongues. But I don't know how it's supposed to come or feel. All the adults seem to pray in tongues. Since I'm not doing that, I figured that I was praying wrong. So I just stopped praying," another youth confided.

HOW SHOULD WE PRAY?

So I opened up a new conversation based on the questions, How should we pray? and Is there a wrong way to pray?

As a teenager, I always found it incredibly difficult (more truthfully, awkward) to share with my parents the things that were going on in my world. I'm not exactly sure why I found this to be the case. But I do know that I wasn't the first teenager who ever felt this way, nor will I be the last. What I did understand, however—what was crystal clear to me—was that my parents were always available when I was ready to talk to them. They made it known that if I ever wanted to discuss anything with them, the door was always open. And they would often encourage me to share with them the happenings in my life. Sometimes, I even took them up on that offer. Other times, I talked to other trusted adults.

After doing youth ministry for about a decade, I realized that the parents of the teenagers I worked with were on the same journey my parents were on when I was a teenager. They just wanted their kids to know that they really loved them and that they would always be there for them.

With that in mind, consider this: What parents would require their child to use only proper language, correct grammar, and an SAT vocabulary when their child wants to talk with them?

"Dearest Mother and Most Venerable Father, may I beseech thy parental presence on this most pleasant of evenings so that I may speaketh to thee about the trouble that lingereth in the depths of this heart of mine?"

Wouldn't you, as the child's parent, say something like, "Why are you talking like that? Just tell me what's on your mind. And know that I love you deeply."

I'm not a parent yet, but I think that I'm correct to assume that most parents want their kids to just talk to them. As they are. No pretenses.

Parents I've worked with, more often than not, simply want to know what's going on in the worlds of their kids. They want their sons and daughters to let them in so that they can be there for them, help them, guide them, teach them, love on them more. They want to share in their children's joy and, if possible, ease their pain. They want to console them in their failures and mishaps and to celebrate with them in their triumphs.

This is how I view the relationship between God and us. God sees through our masks, pretenses, facades, and all of our fancy words. God sees through our babbling and our vague attempts to impress God and those around us who may be listening to us pray.

"Why are you talking to me like that? Just tell me what's on your mind. And know that I love you deeply."

But sometimes it's hard getting started.

So when someone asks me, "How am I supposed to pray?" I often give them one or two "formulaic" (three if you count the Lord's Prayer) prayers that I learned from various youth pastors to help them get going.

PRAYER METHODS

An example of this kind of prayer is the five-finger prayer, where we begin with our thumb. Since it is closest to us, we pray for those who are nearest and dearest to us. The index finger, which we use to point, reminds us to pray for those who teach and instruct us and others. The next finger, which is the tallest of our fingers, reminds us to pray for those who are in authority—local leaders, our bosses, national leaders, and so on. The ring finger, which is often viewed as the weakest, reminds us to pray for those who may be in trouble or suffering. Finally, the pinky finger reminds us of our smallness in relation to God's greatness. So this is the time that we pray for ourselves.

Another pattern prayer is the ACTS prayer. We begin by praying words of *adoration* for and to God. Then we spend time in *confession,* confessing to God our shortcomings. Next we pray prayers of *thanksgiving,* reminding ourselves that all of our blessings come from God. Finally, we pray prayers of *supplication,* in which we ask God to help us and others in life's journey.

When I share these kinds of prayer methods with others, it's always with the caveat that they are only tools designed to help us begin to pray regularly and often. They're not rules for how to pray, nor are they the only ways to pray.

COMMUNICATING WITH GOD

Prayer, above all things, is an act of communication. It is about strengthening our relationship with God. So there really are no "A+B+C=The Best Prayer in the World" type of formulas.

More than anything, prayer has been a relationship strengthener for me. Remember that through Christ's death and resurrection, a loving covenant has been made between God and us. And relationships live or die on how well (and how often) we communicate.

Think about the way we communicate with our loved ones—our spouse, parents, friends, siblings, and so forth.

We may talk about the most random of things that have no bearing in context during the drive home.

We may get into giggle fits, hoping to God we can hold the food in our mouths over a meal at In-N-Out. (For you non-Californians, In-N-Out is the best burger joint in the world.)

We may have a heart-to-heart—as difficult (and necessary) as it may be—quietly over a cup of coffee hoping no one else in the cafe is eavesdropping.

Our conversations can be silly. Or they can be serious. Sometimes, they can be spontaneous and beautifully random.

Other times, we set aside a certain time of the week to make sure that we communicate and interact with one another—like a "date night."

What I'm trying to get at is more than being caught up with how to pray the "right" way, it's more important that we simply remember to pray.

Sure, when we pray, we could make sure that we pray prayers in public to show off our impressive vocabulary and impeccable grammar. But as Christ said, that's probably all we'd get out of those prayers—the compliments of people who actually notice our mad oratorical skills.

But seriously, who likes show-offs? Especially when people are showing off their relationships. For some singles out there, for example, Valentine's Day is the worst day of the year because everyone else seems to be showing off their relationship.

"Look how happy we are!"

"We're so in love!"

And you want to ask: Are you trying to convince the world you're in love or are you trying to convince each other that you're in love? Because if you need a nationally recognized day to be reminded to celebrate your love, how much in love are you?

In a similar way, if you need a public platform to pray to God, how strong is your relationship with God? Are you in love with God or in love with yourself?

We have public declarations to let people know that we're in love with each other: weddings, hand-holding, nauseating PDAs (public displays of affection), his-and-her matching clothing.

And we have public declarations to let people know that we're in love with God: Going to church. Bumper stickers. Church-branded apparel. Mission and service projects in the community.

Likewise, church and corporate worship are vital to our faith formation. Prayer groups, worship services, and Bible studies help us continue on our faith journey. But it's in the private moments, in the just-God-and-me moments, behind closed doors, where intimacy happens and our relationship with God grows and is strengthened.

And I don't think that you need me or anyone else, to tell you how to talk with and pray to God in those intimate, private moments.

Spontaneously, randomly, intently, and purposefully may we continue to deepen our relationship with our Creator by regularly engaging, communing, talking, crying, and laughing with God through our prayers.

QUESTIONS

1. Why does Jesus say that we shouldn't practice our religion in front of people in order to draw their attention (Matthew 6:1)?

2. What are we to make of group prayer, in light of verses 5-7? How should we approach public prayer?

3. Why should we pray in a "secret place"? How might God reward us for doing this (verse 6)?

4. What does it mean to pray with "empty words" (verse 7)? Why is it important to remember that God knows what we need before we ask (verse 8)? Why ask at all if God already knows?

5. What is the significance of the Lord's Prayer (verses 9-13)? What role should it play in public prayer? What about in private prayer?

6. What do we mean when we pray, "Bring in your kingdom" (verse 10)? What role does prayer play in accomplishing this?

7. Why would we ask God not to lead us into temptation (verse 13)?

8. Is God making our forgiveness contingent on our forgiving others (verses 14-15)? What are some potential pitfalls of this interpretation?

9. What are the positive aspects of prayer methods and patterns (for example, the five-finger prayer or the ACTS prayer)? What are the cons?

10. How does prayer facilitate the intimacy of our relationship with God?

11. How does one find the appropriate balance between regimented prayer and completely spontaneous prayer?

12. What kinds of prayer have you found to be most effective?

13. What are some ways in which you can make your prayer life more vital? How can other believers help with this?

3

ANSWERS TO PRAYER
LEARNING TO RECOGNIZE THE UNEXPECTED

SCRIPTURE
MATTHEW 7:7-11; LUKE 11:5-8; MATTHEW 21:18-22

MATTHEW 7:7-11

[7]"Ask, and you will receive. Search, and you will find. Knock, and the door will be opened to you. [8]For everyone who asks, receives. Whoever seeks, finds. And to everyone who knocks, the door is opened. [9]Who among you will give your children a stone when they ask for bread? [10]Or give them a snake when they ask for fish? [11]If you who are evil know how to give good gifts to your children, how much more will your heavenly Father give good things to those who ask him."

LUKE 11:5-8

[5]He also said to them, "Imagine that one of you has a friend and you go to that friend in the middle of the night. Imagine saying, 'Friend,

loan me three loaves of bread [6]because a friend of mine on a journey has arrived and I have nothing to set before him.' [7]Imagine further that he answers from within the house, 'Don't bother me. The door is already locked, and my children and I are in bed. I can't get up to give you anything.' [8]I assure you, even if he wouldn't get up and help because of his friendship, he will get up and give his friend whatever he needs because of his friend's brashness."

MATTHEW 21:18-22

[18]Early in the morning as Jesus was returning to the city, he was hungry. [19]He saw a fig tree along the road, but when he came to it, he found nothing except leaves. Then he said to it, "You'll never again bear fruit!" The fig tree dried up at once.

[20]When the disciples saw it, they were amazed. "How did the fig tree dry up so fast?" they asked.

[21]Jesus responded, "I assure you that if you have faith and don't doubt, you will not only do what was done to the fig tree. You will even say to this mountain, 'Be lifted up and thrown into the lake.' And it will happen. [22]If you have faith, you will receive whatever you pray for.

INSIGHT AND IDEAS

I had a huge crush on a girl during my tenth-grade year. I didn't know what love was, but I figured that this must be it.

I prayed that God would make a certain girl (we'll call her Lois) like me. After all, her liking me back was a pretty big and important detail. I prayed for about a week but felt nothing happening. So I asked for a sign. I prayed that the next day, if Lois was the first person to say hi to me before band, that would be God's sign that she liked me and that I should ask her out.

The following day, I stood very nervously outside of the band room. When I saw my friends approaching, I hid so that they wouldn't say hi to me. The bell was going to ring soon, and she wasn't here yet. I was getting worried.

"Hey, Joe!" Except it wasn't a girl's voice.

I was so worried about Lois's whereabouts that I wasn't paying attention to the door and didn't see this buffoon walk in. Did he not know the plan?

"Nooo! You ruined everything!" I yelled.

"Dude, you need to calm down," he replied.

It was at that moment that Lois walked in.

"Hey, Joe!"

All was ruined.

"God, why don't you ever answer my prayers?" I asked as I sulked back into my seat.

'UNANSWERED' PRAYER

Over the years, I've heard many people share with me that one of the reasons they give up on praying is that "it never works" and God never seems to answer.

Part of the problem may be that some of us have limited prayer to just asking God for things. After days, weeks, and months of ignoring God, God becomes the go-to person when we need something. And nobody likes those who call only when they need something.

We also may feel entitled. After all, we go to church, we try to not curse during the week, we try to be nice to that really annoying neighbor kid, we sit through the pastor's sermon and stay awake, and we give money. We do all that stuff for God; so God should, we figure, at the very least, return the favor and answer our prayers.

Perhaps, to some of us, there's not much of a difference between God and a genie, except that God doesn't always grant our wishes. We read passages where Jesus says things like, "Ask, and you will receive. . . . For everyone who asks, receives. Whoever seeks, finds. And to everyone who knocks, the door is opened" (Matthew 7:7a-8).

And we argue, "I asked! I searched! I knocked! But nothing! What gives?"

Rick Warren tweeted once that there are "six ways God answers prayers: Yes; No; Not yet; You be the answer; Trust me; and Are you kidding me?"

Let's start with the last one, because it's my favorite. I'm sure that God often hears my prayers and asks, "Are you kidding me?" I think that Lois is one example.

Was I really praying that God would make someone *like* me? What about free will? Lois might've thought that I was repulsive. Why would God have made her like me even if she hated me?

Not even the genie from *Aladdin* would do that. ("I can't make anybody fall in love with anyone else," the genie explains before turning into a pair of lips and kissing Aladdin.)

The truth is, I believe that there are times when God says, "No."

There are places in the Bible where people prayed and God said, "No."

Paul pleaded with God three times for the thorn to leave him alone (2 Corinthians 12:8-9).

David begged God that his newborn baby would live (2 Samuel 12:15-17).

Jesus prayed that, if possible, God would "take this cup of suffering away from" him (Luke 22:42).

Sometimes God doesn't grant what we pray for, and we don't always know the reason.

REASONS GOD SAYS NO

God may say no because what we're asking may be harmful for us. If a boy were to ask for a poisonous snake, we wouldn't get it for him (at least, I hope not). Perhaps what we're asking for could cause us great harm, so God says no.

I used to take our family dog out for walks on a regular route that included a sidewalk on a large and busy street. The dog would try her darnedest to get a sniff of the grass six lanes across the street (talk about grass being greener on the other side). I would have to pull hard on the leash dozens of times so that she wouldn't get smashed by the cars zooming by. (Why I never took a different route is beyond me. I guess I'm a creature of habit.)

All my dog could see was new, unsniffed, and unmarked grass that she desperately needed to get to. But I could see more, like all the cars going fifty miles per hour on all six lanes of the street. I wouldn't be a good dog owner if I were to let my dog try to dodge traffic just to pee on the grass on the other side.

Perhaps sometimes, because we're so focused on what we feel we need, we miss the possible dangers around us. But God doesn't. God sees what lies ahead, and maybe that's a reason God says no.

God's also not going to allow us to avoid personal responsibility. God's not going to "save" us from getting a bad grade when we had partied all night and went to class the following morning on zero sleep, only to remember that there's an exam that day. Oops!

Yes, we pray. We pray hard. We bargain. But we still have to live with the consequences of not studying.

If we're unfaithful in a relationship, I don't think God will honor the prayer "Please don't let my partner find out I cheated!"

Sometimes we don't know what we're asking for or the impact of our request. But God does. So God tells us no. And we simply have to trust.

Other times, we may not be ready for the things we ask for. Looking back, I am glad that I got my first lead pastor position at the age of 31, not at the age of 26. I felt I was ready at 26, and I prayed and told God I was ready. But I simply wasn't. At 26, I was still brash, immature, and too outspoken (in a bad way). Five years made a lot of difference.

So God often says, "Not yet," which often goes hand in hand with, "Trust me." Actually, *yes, no, not yet,* and *you be the answer*—they all go hand in hand with "trust me," trusting that God is in control and, despite how we may feel, trusting that God knows what's going on.

WHEN GOD SAYS YES

But God does say yes to our prayers. It's just that sometimes, we don't see it, perhaps because we're wanting God to respond in an obviously miraculous way. Or instantaneously.

There's a joke about a priest on top of a roof during a great flood. A man comes by in a boat and says, "Get in!" The priest replies, "No, son, I have faith in God to save me."

The floods get higher, and another boat comes by. And the guy in the boat yells, "Father! Get in!"

"No, my son," the priest replies. "God will save me. I have faith in God."

The water is now up to his neck. A helicopter throws down a ladder, and a man yells for the priest to climb up.

"No, my child," the priest yells back, "God will save me!"

The priest arrives in heaven after not having survived the flood, and he's a little peeved.

"What's wrong?" God asks.

"God, I had faith that you'd save me. But you let me drown!"

"What more do you want from me?" God says. "I sent you two boats and a helicopter!"

Sometimes we miss God's response because we're looking for something bigger. Grander. More miraculous. So we don't notice the person who calls to check on how we're doing when we tell God we're struggling.

We're oblivious to the person who brings us a casserole for dinner when we're worried about eating, because we don't particularly like casserole and we've been praying for steak.

We miss that God's healing presence is flowing through doctors and nurses when we're praying for someone to get well.

I keep a prayer journal where I write down a lot of my prayers. After a year, I go back and read the prayers; and I'm consistently surprised at how many prayers God really answered. But it's hardly ever the way I expected.

I once prayed to God that a person I didn't like would leave the church, because I felt that the person was making my job more difficult. That person never left the church, but God made my heart bigger and opened my eyes to see more than the tension between the two of us. We ended up working on a number of ministries together without any problems.

How many of your prayers has God answered, but you just didn't see it because it wasn't what you had expected?

WHEN YOU'RE PART OF THE ANSWER

Finally, "You be the answer." In this scenario, we become partners with God. What a concept, that God would collaborate with us, even with our faults and shortcomings!

But that has always been God's MO: using a murderer and a stutterer to be God's voice, using a con man to be the father of a nation, using a murderous adulterer as one of Israel's most beloved kings, using a young girl to bring forth the promise we sing about during Christmas.

God works through our faults, shortcomings, and weaknesses. God uses the weak to lead the strong. So when we pray, we may sometimes find ourselves in a situation that the disciples found themselves in.

Jesus was preaching to the crowd, when the disciples came to him and said, "Send them away so that they can go to the surrounding countryside and villages and buy something to eat for themselves" (Mark 6:36).

Jesus' response?

"*You* give them something to eat" (Mark 6:37, emphasis mine).

47

Similarly, there's a great story out there about someone who was complaining about God when he learned of all the hungry people in the world.

"How can you do nothing about all of the people starving in the world?" the man demanded.

"I did do something," God replied. "I created you."

We have a God who chooses to work with us to make this world a better place. Therefore, prayer needs action.

If you pray for a job, you can't just sit around and hope that the phone rings with a lucrative job offer. You pray for a job while you're actively job hunting.

You pray that God will do something about the homeless people in your community, while you and your church serve the people you're praying for.

Prayer needs action.

God will use you to answer not only some of your own prayers, but you may very well be the answer to someone else's prayers.

God is always answering our prayers; so let's continuously pray, knowing that God is always with us and for us.

And may we learn to recognize the answers.

QUESTIONS

1. What is the difference between asking, searching, and knocking (Matthew 7:7)?

2. Jesus says that whoever asks, receives (Matthew 7:8). Why didn't Jesus qualify this statement?

3. In light of Matthew 7:8, why do some prayers still seem to go unanswered?

4. Why does Jesus seem to be comparing God to a person who doesn't want his friend bothering him in the middle of the night (Luke 11:5-8)?

5. What is Jesus telling us about prayer in Luke 11:5-8?

6. Why does Jesus curse the fig tree (Matthew 21:19)? Why does he later connect this action with prayer (Matthew 21:22)?

7. How do we get the kind of faith Jesus talks about in Matthew 21:21?

8. How does the way we view our relationship with God affect the way we look at prayer and God's answers to prayer?

9. How do we balance "waiting on God" with participating in the answers to our own prayers?

10. Have you ever kept a prayer journal? In what ways did it help you recognize ways God answered your prayers?

11. How do you know when to stop praying for something?

4

LISTENING TO GOD
THE OTHER PART OF PRAYER

SCRIPTURE
1 KINGS 19:8-13

[8]Elijah got up, ate and drank, and went refreshed by that food for forty days and nights until he arrived at Horeb, God's mountain. [9]There he went into a cave and spent the night.

The Lord's word came to him and said, "Why are you here, Elijah?"

[10]Elijah replied, "I've been very passionate for the Lord God of heavenly forces because the Israelites have abandoned your covenant. They have torn down your altars, and they have murdered your prophets with the sword. I'm the only one left, and now they want to take my life too!"

[11]The Lord said, "Go out and stand at the mountain before the Lord. The Lord is passing by." A very strong wind tore through the mountains and broke apart the stones before the Lord. But the

LORD wasn't in the wind. After the wind, there was an earthquake. But the LORD wasn't in the earthquake. [12]After the earthquake, there was a fire. But the LORD wasn't in the fire. After the fire, there was a sound. Thin. Quiet. [13]When Elijah heard it, he wrapped his face in his coat. He went out and stood at the cave's entrance. A voice came to him and said, "Why are you here, Elijah?"

INSIGHT AND IDEAS

In prayer, listening to God is just as important as pouring out our hearts to God. In 1 Kings 19, Elijah is inside a cave, waiting for God to appear. At first, there's a powerful wind that tears the mountains apart and shatters rocks. Then there's an earthquake. After the earthquake, there's a fire. But God isn't to be found in any of those things.

I would've totally been expecting God to be in one of those three elements. Especially the wind, because it just makes sense that such an awesome God would show up in such a powerful way. But that's not where Elijah found God.

"After the fire, there was a sound. Thin. Quiet. When Elijah heard it, he wrapped his face in his coat. He went out and stood at the cave's entrance" (verses 12b-13b). Oftentimes, that's how God's voice seems to be described: as a whisper.

I think it's perfectly reasonable to ask, "Why?" Wouldn't it be more beneficial for both God and us if God were to use more obvious ways to get our attention?

From an early age, we figure out that if we want to be heard, we need to be loud. Of course, the adults in our lives try to teach us otherwise. But we still know that we can get their attention by being loud. When we're in a debate or an argument, and we're losing, some of us resort to the notion, "whoever is loudest wins." Many sports radio DJs and news pundits rely on being loud and obnoxious, because they know that it increases their potential for high ratings.

A WHISPER IS EASY TO MISS

A small, still, thin, and quiet voice can be easy to miss or ignore; because there are so many things competing for our attention and so much noise in our lives today. I have music playing in the background whether I'm working, driving, exercising, falling asleep, or simply bored. If I'm at home, it's not unusual to have the TV on as background noise while I'm playing a game on my iPad (with the sound on) and also listening for the text message "bing" from a friend. A whisper can be easy to miss.

Surely, God could use a different, louder method to get our attention. A loud, booming voice calling our name. A roaring wind that leaves debris spelling out our name on our front lawn. Or a fire. A burning bush like what God did for Moses. It would be so much easier to recognize God's voice and presence in those things than in a whisper.

IT'S POSSIBLE TO IGNORE AN EARTHQUAKE

I live in Southern California. Every once in a while, someone will mention that we're overdue for the "big one." I am, of course, talking about earthquakes. (I also lived in Hawaii. Yes, I know, woe is me. And every once in a while, someone over there would mention that we were overdue for "the big one," referring to hurricanes.)

One day I was hanging out with a friend who had recently moved out to Southern California from Virginia. We were talking when the earth slightly rolled. It lasted about three seconds. It probably registered well below 4.0 on the Richter scale. I didn't think much of it, because small earthquakes aren't that much of a sticking point with most Californians. They're so common that, when they occur, we usually just roll with it and go on with the rest of our day. Recently, one part of Southern California experienced three or four small earthquakes within a day, and no one really freaked out. Such is life here, I suppose.

After the small earthquake, I looked up at my friend to continue our conversation, only to see that she was shocked and terrified. She was gripping the table with her now-white knuckles. Meanwhile, everyone else in the coffee shop continued on as though nothing had happened.

"What's wrong with you? Are you all right?" I asked.

"What's wrong with *me*? What's wrong with *you*? How can you guys act like nothing happened?"

"Oh, that? That was nothing. Really. You'll get used to it soon enough."

She never did.

Years later, she would move back to Virginia, only to experience another earthquake around 4.0 on the Richter scale. While people on the East Coast were flipping out and posting all sorts of pictures and status updates on social media (like the meme of a lawn chair tipped on the ground with the words "Never forget" and "8/23/11" above it), Californians were wondering, "Why are they making such a big deal over such a small earthquake? That's just a stroll in the park here."

What I'm getting at is, while we think that it would be easy to miss or ignore a whisper, it turns out that it can be just as easy to ignore loud and obvious things. Like earthquakes. Or ask those who live next to an airport. Eventually, they get used to the airplanes roaring over their houses, shaking everything in it.

Even with the burning bush, I like to believe that Moses didn't realize what was going on at first. Perhaps he thought that it was simply a bush that had caught on fire, which might have been a common occurrence in such a climate. (Californians, unfortunately, know all about brush fires, as they are an annual horrifying event.) Moses was probably gathering his things to move on to the next grazing area. Only this time, he lingered just a little longer. That was when he realized that something wasn't right. The bush was on fire, but it wasn't burning up. Who knows? Maybe that bush had been on fire for days before Moses had noticed it.

WHY GOD WHISPERS

Maybe one of the reasons God chooses to speak to us in a small, still voice—a whisper—is because of the intimate nature of a whisper. In order to whisper something to someone, we need to be very close to the person, both physically and emotionally. Not just anyone can whisper in our ear, nor do we usually whisper in a complete stranger's ear. And if a stranger leans in to whisper to us, we instinctively pull away; because it's an offensive violation of our personal space.

If someone doesn't know how to properly whisper, he or she may lose that privilege forever. Have you ever had someone get so close to you to whisper something that his or her lips touched your ear? Or what about those who use too much breath in their whisper and leave you moist after they're done? (I wanted information from you. I didn't ask for a kiss.)

Not everyone knows us well enough to whisper into our ears. That's why we whisper sweet nothings into the ears of our lover and allow only that person to do the same to us.

Sometimes it takes a whisper to really get our attention.

My parents are kind of loud. When I was growing up, they yelled and nagged at me all the time—so much so that it became very easy to tune them out. I would simply nod and walk away in a respectful manner. But when they were really upset—when I was in real big trouble—they wouldn't yell. Instead, they'd lower their voices. It was quiet but forceful. When they did this, I knew I'd better listen; because I had really messed up.

It's why we preachers often lower our voices, instead of shouting, when we have an important point to drive home. We want people on the edge of their seats, really listening to us.

When we know that someone is going to whisper something, we really want to hear what he or she has to say. It could be big, exciting news or something that's juicy and forbidden. Either way, it's exciting when a friend says, "I have to tell you something." Then, before leaning in closer to us—which instinctively makes us lean closer to them—he or she looks around to make sure that no one else is there to hear.

That's why I think God chooses to whisper to us in that "thin, quiet" voice. It's more intimate. It's more personal. Sure, a whisper is easy to overlook. But once we learn to hear God's quiet voice, it becomes hard to ignore.

The more we commune with God, the more familiar we become with God's voice. In any relationship, the more we spend time with a person, the more we get to know that person. That's why best friends can finish each other's sentences. It's why married couples can communicate with just their eyes.

I shared with you earlier that it's not unusual for me to be surrounded by all sorts of noise. As I am writing this, I'm sitting at my favorite Starbucks, listening to the music playing in my earphones as well as the music playing inside the store. The people near me are talking so loudly that I'm forced to eavesdrop during the breaks in the music.

THAT'S ENOUGH!

If every moment of our lives is this noisy and cluttery, how can we possibly hear anything, let alone God's quiet voice? Psalm 46:10 says: "That's enough! Now know that I am God.!

"That's enough" works on so many levels for me. That's enough of all the noise that pollutes your ears, mind, heart, and soul. That's enough of all your complaints and worries. That's enough of all your prayer lists, requests, and supplications.

"That's enough! Now know that I am God!"

May we continue deepening our relationship with God through prayer. May we take moments from our days, every day, where we can quiet our busy minds and listen for God's thin, quiet voice.

"That's enough! Now know that I am God!"

QUESTIONS

1. How do you imagine God's Word coming to Elijah (verse 9)?

2. Why is Elijah desperate to hear from God (verse 10)?

3. What's the significance of the wind, earthquake, and fire (verses 11-12)?

4. Why does Elijah wrap his face in his coat when he hears God's voice (verse 13)?

5. What is the difference between God's voice in verse 9 and in verse 13? What is different about Elijah?

6. Why does God often speak with a quiet voice when it would be much easier to get our attention by being louder and more obvious?

7. What steps should one take to hear God's voice more clearly?

8. How is communicating with God like communicating with a close friend? How is it different?

9. Which do you find to be easier—talking to God or listening to God? Why?

10. What struggles do you have with regular prayer? How do you overcome these struggles?

63

CONVERGE

Bible Studies

WOMEN OF THE BIBLE
by James A. Harnish
9781426771545

OUR COMMON SINS
by Dottie Escobedo-Frank
9781426768989

WHO YOU ARE IN CHRIST
by Shane Raynor
9781426771538

SHARING THE GOSPEL
by Curtis Zackery
9781426771569

KINGDOM BUILDING
by Grace Biskie
9781426771576

RECLAIMING ANGER
by David Dorn
9781426771552

THREE GIFTS, ONE CHRIST
by Katie Dawson
9781426778278

And more to come.

Don't miss any
of the upcoming
titles in the
CONVERGE
Bible Studies series:

Abingdon Press™

BKM13660007 PACP01383970-01

CPSIA information can be obtained at www.ICGtesting.com
Printed in the USA
LVOW12s0051060514

384502LV00003B/4/P

9 781426 778254